meanwhile the

EARTH

MEANWHILE THE EARTH

Poems from Cougar Creek

Stacie Smith

Shanti Arts Publishing
Brunswick, Maine

Meanwhile the Earth
Poems from Cougar Creek

Published by Shanti Arts Publishing

Cover and interior design
by Shanti Arts Designs

Cover image by Stacie Smith
Interior fern images from Flickr /
Biodiversity Heritage Library

Shanti Arts LLC
Brunswick, Maine
www.shantiarts.com

Printed in the United States of America

ISBN: 978-1-947067-54-7

LCCN: 2018909519

for Jan and Jack

"Who? Who? Who?"

— Great Horned Owl

Inland a few miles from the Pacific Ocean, at the confluence of two salmon spawning streams, is a place called Cougar Creek by those who know and love it. I have known and loved it for nearly twenty years. Old growth fir, broad leaf and vine maple, alder, cedar, hemlock, salal, various ferns, huckleberry, salmonberry, trillium, nettle, equisetum, skunk cabbage, snails, slugs, frogs, owls, hawks, herons, eagles, hummingbirds, thrushes, coyotes, rabbits, chipmunks, elk, bear, cougar, salamanders, snakes, all manner of insects, and mosses, mushrooms, and fungi thrive there; if I were better versed in botany and biology, I could fill many pages with lists of species that co-exist in this special spot. The air is moist and clean and fragrant. Aside from birdsong and wind and the sound of the downhill stream, Cougar Creek is a quiet place.

In the mid-1970s, a group of friends went together to purchase this thirty-plus-acre parcel of land, formerly a small farm, as a retreat place from their work and family lives in the Willamette Valley just an hour further inland. The property had one structure, an old farmhouse, which is now moldering into the ground thanks to gravity, neglect, and encroaching blackberries. A few fruit trees and a couple of rows of very old blueberry bushes are still productive. Irrigation water for the overgrown garden comes from the creek. Drinking water — the best on Earth — comes from a hillside spring.

In the 1970s and '80s, adjacent properties were heavily logged, but Cougar Creek was protected from that devastation by its new owners. Massive replanting of trees, both evergreen and deciduous, has been a project priority from the beginning. Of the original group of land-owners, one family is still engaged and steadfast in its commitment to stewardship of Cougar Creek.

As a friend of two of the original and principal stewards, I first visited the land in the fall of 1998. I made the trip solo, approaching the place at dusk, guided by my friends' directions to the cabin perched high above the narrow road: "Find the big, old maple tree by the parking spot, and look for the little wooden dolphin sign nailed to the tree trunk. The dolphin's nose points to the trail up to the cabin."

I found the trail. It was long and steep with switch-backs flanked by sword fern and salal and huckleberry. By the very last of the day's light, I found the cabin, a hobbit-like structure with a heavy hand-hewn wooden door. I unlocked the door, stepped inside, and immediately felt at home, welcome, secure. I lit a fire in the vintage woodstove, settled in, and listened to the night sounds. I was instantly in love with the place.

The poems in this offering were written during my stays at Cougar Creek. They are little exhalations, little evocations of that fecund and beautiful place and my relationship with it. My gratitude to Cougar Creek — with its majestic, constant, and healing energy — knows no bounds. These poems are little love-songs to that beloved place, my way of saying thank you.

Stacie Smith
Corvallis, Oregon
February 2017

I

Raccoon digging for liquid gold
on the roof inches above my head.
I fall asleep to the sound
of angry bees.

I dream amazing dreams,
wake up to beauty
buzzing in the air,
bees in my hair!

II

Deep dark woods,
unfamiliar place.

Moss cloaks it all
and I am not afraid.

As the sun goes down
shadows move to cloak me.

Alone in the deep dark woods,
I am not afraid.

III

My ambition
went out for a stroll
and hasn't come back.

I sit here
waiting for her return
but I think she's gone
for good.

IV

Wind in the grass
Music in the stream
Shadow on the page
Life is but a dream

V

amber
candle
shining
creek
rushing
night bird
winging
heart
beating
eyes
seeing
shadows
dancing
ears
hearing
earth
breathing
silence
singing

VI

It is wild,
this world at war
and I notice
the absence
of honey bees.
I study the pioneers
for stories of strength
and they inspire
but that was then
and long ago.
Give me a sky
of locusts
any day.

VII

Friends
die
and
so
will
I

VIII

A reputable source tells me
appearance is deity's body
thought is deity's mind
sound is deity's voice.
Since receiving this news
I wander around all day
watching
wondering
listening

IX

Time —
what is it?
My unknowing is vast.
Answers twinkle at me
from the edge of space.

X

Clouds the shape of horses' manes.
Burdock. Blackberry.
Tall wild grasses sway
in the shifting breeze.
Cougar Creek splashes down
and down and down
over stone and fallen branch.
Birdcall. Black fly buzz.
Crystal rainbows flash
from a bead of morning dew.

XI

I am here for now
noticing this fact of sight.
What greater miracle?
I see! I am here
for a moment only!
Tomorrow my light
could be extinguished
by the slightest breeze!

XII

— for Jack

We surf the Data Sea
clutching a plastic mouse.
Look! We can find out
anything, any time!
Meanwhile the Earth
deletes species.

XIII

— Mothers' Day 2002

She's alive!
Her Bleeding Heart
Fiddlehead Fern
Hummingbird, Wren
Wasp and Snail!

She's alive!
Her water like music
flows down and down
her green and glowing
mountainside.

XIV

My mother said
"It is one thing
to say you are
ready to die,
quite another
to actually
say goodbye."

XV

So you think
you know your way home

but along the way
you forget your name.

What then?

XVI

A bird whistles
its flute-like upward trill.

Daylight fades.
Flame in the woodstove.

Song in the downhill stream.
My hand as it moves

across the page.
My breathing in and out

and beyond my door
the exhalations of stone.

XVII

Held hostage by the day,
all exits barred.
Besieged by the chaos
of a world at war.
Meanwhile, spotted cows
browse the emerald fields.

XVIII

Through branches of alder
vine maple and fir
I watch the dew-covered field
where blackberry wins its war.

Sunlight brightens the green
the scarlet, the gold.
Meanwhile frightened men
sharpen their swords.

XIX

— 9/11

Today the towers fell.
The star-shaped hub
of military might
was stunned.

Tonight the crickets sing.
The stars are clear
this early autumn night —
two worlds in one.

XX

Everyone around me
these days
whether of this view
or of that
brandishes their
convictions
like a sword.

XXI

Red-tailed hawk
high above
screeches once, twice —
"See me! See me!"

I watch it circle
once, twice —
then it glides out of sight,
my heart its prey.

XXII

. . . the soft sound of flame,
the murmur of thoughts
as they slowly hush to hear
the creek, the bird, the wind . . .

XXIII

Outside the window
a bird calls its single note —
a drop of water
in a still pool.

News of the human world
clamors in my heart's mind —
a drop of water
in a still pool.

XXIV

I'm not impressed
by the noise we make.
Not the news.
Not the high notes
or the low notes
of the opera
or the blues.
Not the news.
But yes the crow.
Yes the spring-fed creek.
Yes the wind.
Yes the silence that sings.

XXV

Today's surprising rain
falls hard from the sky,
pulled to the thirsty ground
like a long lost love.
See how the fading green responds,
lifts itself up and up
and all the dusty leaves
begin to glisten and glow.
See how even the memory of drought
is gently washed away . . .

XXVI

Huge poem
beginning at dawn —
bird chorus sounding
like glass flutes
high in the canopy!
Rumi would know
how to say it
but I can only
open my eyes and
listen with my heart's
many tiny ears.

XXVII

The Swainson's Thrush —
have you heard its voice?
Where I live these days
the summer air throbs
with its song.

What is the message
in its upward trilling call?
Is she saying "this place is mine!"
or "where are you?"
or "I am here! I am here!
I am here!"

XXVIII

Coho in Elk Horn Creek
aim upstream
ponderous massive and wild
waiting in the deep dark pool
until the time is right
to turn toward the confluence
with Cougar Creek and then
head up and up and up
toward the place of their beginning
where no one is there to see.

XXIX

— for Jack

Maybe from where you are —
if you are anywhere
or nowhere, or who knows
— everywhere —
some light from that place
might rain down on us
or shine or fall
or somehow help us out
stuck as we are here
in this web of unknowing.

I thought about you
as I walked the creek-side trail
to the Buddha who now wears
a crown and cloak of moss.
I wondered how you are
if you are anything or nothing
or who knows
— everything.

XXX

Clouds of sword fern pollen
backlit and golden fill the air.
Alder leaves drop
like bright rain.

Black fly buzz mingles
with sounds of the downhill stream.
Vine maple branches rattle
in young September's wind.

News of the world
doesn't enter this place
but I hear it anyway.
It's in my blood and bones

so it comes with me
on the trail to the spring.
It thirsts like I do
for the silence that sings.

XXXI

Yesterday's sunlight guided my hand to you,
plump blueberry heavy on the branch.
This morning you swim in my bowl of cream.

Do I owe you an apology?
Am I sorry to be swallowing the sun?
You know I too am food for the One.

XXXII

Vine maple leaves unfurl
as they have done
since long before this place
first saved my life
by teaching me to listen
and to breathe.

A ruby-throated hummingbird
darts chittering and flashing
inches from my face
then zooms away, erasing
what I might have thought
was big enough to say.

XXXIII

— birthday wish at 71

I wish for my remaining days
to explore the ways complexity
can be undone.

As for the nights
I have no control —
let dreams recalibrate my little goals.

I blow the many candles out
and wish with all my mortal might
to live whatever's left of me — right.

XXXIV

A strange eagerness
pushes me onto the road.

A kind of weightless wonder
pulls me away

from all I thought
I knew.

XXXV

Nothing left to say.
The crow calls
its familiar boast.
All the smaller birds
fly from its path.

Nothing left to do.
I look at the ground
and see my shadow
merge with the shadows
of crows.

XXXVI

I decline to rage
against the dying of the light.

I've seen Coho
in the spawning stream.

They show me
there's another way to fight.

I'll harness rage and sorrow
and I'll try to harness fright.

I'll let them lead me
toward the light.

Have men who think
they own the world

seen Coho
in the spawning stream?

Have they ever seen
the Salmon's dignity and might?

I've seen Coho
in the spawning stream.

Nothing stops their movement
toward the light.

XXXVII

some things feel
too sacred to say
but i'll try anyway:
those bodies
undulating
dark and wild
pulled upstream
by lust and memory.
how must it feel
to be driven
by such certainty?
when i first saw
coho spawn

in cougar creek
i didn't believe
my eyes.
fearful awe
came over me.
that vision altered me
stopped my breath
my heart
repaired my sight
recalibrated
— utterly —
my sense
of what is right

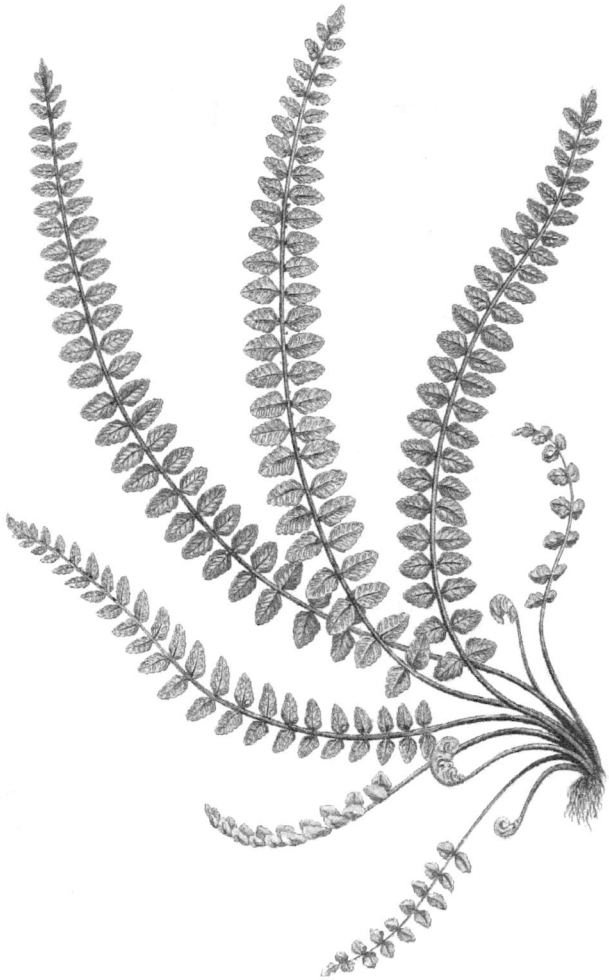

Artist and poet Stacie Smith was born in Salem, Oregon, in 1945. She is a fourth-generation Oregonian whose maternal great-great-grandparents came west on the Oregon Trail. Stacie grew up in the Willamette Valley and in the mid-1960s studied writing with William Stafford at Lewis and Clark College in Portland. Stacie currently resides in her hometown, Eugene, Oregon. This is her second book of poetry.

SHANTI ARTS

nature · art · spirit

Please visit us on online

to browse our entire book catalog,

including additional poetry collections and fiction,

books on travel, nature, healing, art,

photography, and more.

shantiarts.com

www.ingramcontent.com/pod-product-compliance
Lightning Source LLC
Chambersburg PA
CBHW060523280326

41933CB00014B/3088